Publisher:

Bumper's Garage, Book 1

Text and illustrations copyright © 2019 by Geoff Holladay.
All rights reserved.

Published by
Long Pull Press, LLC
PO Box 1410
Lamesa, Texas 79331

No part of this book may be reproduced or transmitted in any form or by any means, electronic or mechanical, including photocopying, recording, or by any information storage and retrieval system, without written premission from the publisher or author.

Printed in China
978-1-7334111-0-3

Contact info@bumpersgarage.com for more information.

To all the real life Bumpers who inspired this story.

- G.H.

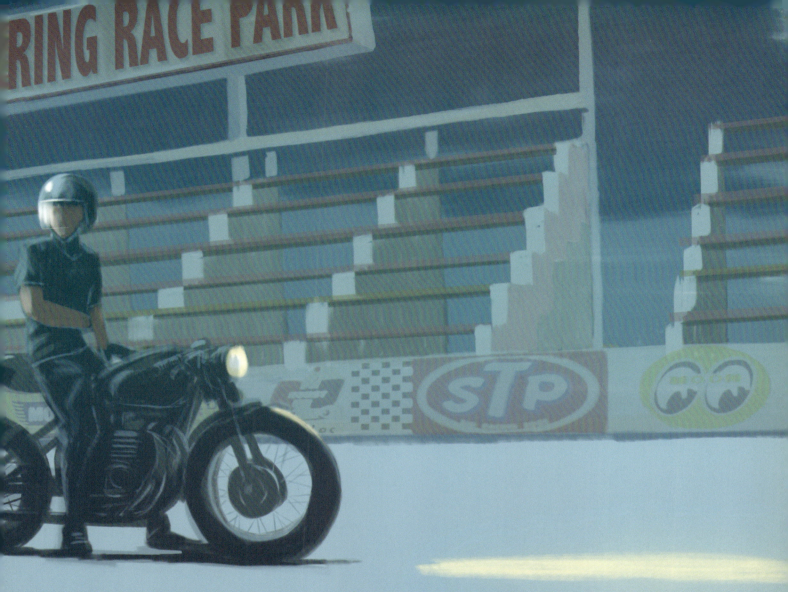

Steve Auburn was a professional racer. He was the fastest kid ever around the track at Leaf Spring Race Park. He waited for the green flag, hands sweating, feet trembling with anticipation.

Actually, he was the fastest person of any age around the track. Nobody came out here anymore, but that didn't stop Steve. Helmet tight, shoelaces tied, the flag dropped! He launched his bike off the line and... rolled to a stop. The only thing stopping him today was his bike chain.

His dad had warned him about riding his bike too hard while he still needed it for his paper route. Now it was broken again, and he still had a lot of work to do.

"Just a little bit more and I'll have... OUCH!" Steve cried, holding his thumb.
"This isn't going to work. I'll never get all these papers delivered on time now."

"DAD! I think its busted for good this time, and I've got a ton of deliveries today."

Startled, his dad slapped a hand over the phone. "What's that buddy? Your bike? Let me take a look."

Steve watched over his dad's shoulder. "Yup, looks like your front cog has a crack in it. That's why the chain keeps popping off. Let's get this loaded up and over to Eli Baumer. He can fix anything."

They pushed his bike up to the front door of an old building. "Dad, are you sure we're at the right place?" Steve asked.

As they walked in, Steve noticed a torn sticker on the door. While he was trying to make sense of what it used to say, his dad rang the bell on the counter. DING!

An old man shuffled in from the shop.
"Yeah, I'm here, what can I do for you?" he said.
"Hey Eli, Steve has a problem with his bike."
Dad winked. "Think you could help him out?"

Eli carefully inspected the bike. "Been a long time, Dean; good to see you've got someone riding shotgun. This front cog seems to have a crack in it. Chain keeps popping off I bet."

"Wow, you were right, dad!" Steve said, sounding amazed.
"Ok buddy," Dad laughed. "You're in good hands now and I need to get back to work. I'll see you at home after you get everything finished up."

The old man opened a door to the biggest shop Steve had ever seen. "What is this place?" he asked. "I bet you've got EVERYTHING!"

Eli and Steve searched through bin after bin in the huge building talking back and forth when, suddenly, Steve noticed an old sign with a clock on it.

"Mr. Baumer, is this thing right? It's almost 11 o'clock!" he said, sounding panicked. "There's no way I can fix my bike and get all these papers delivered on time!"
With a huge grin Eli said "Just a minute, Steve. We've got one more place to look."

He opened a side door and led Steve into a small garage. Next to a workbench and a lift were three mysterious objects covered with old canvas tarps. "This is my special garage. I don't get out here as much as I used to, but I think one of my toys might be able to help us out."

He walked over to one of the tarps and with a grand gesture pulled it away to reveal a motorcycle with deep black paint and glistening chrome.

Eli swung a leg over the bike and put his foot on the big v-twin engine's kickstart. Close the choke, tickle the carbs, pull the valve lifter, kick, kick, VROMP! With an explosive cough the engine fired up and settled into a low, thumping idle.

"Helmet up and hop on Steve! We'll get those papers delivered quicker than a cat can lick its paw. And from now on, you can just call me Ol Bumper."

Steve and Bumper raced through downtown on the old twin getting all the deliveries made even earlier than usual. Steve had never had so much fun. The sounds coming from the big chrome pipes were like thunder bouncing off everything they passed. Steve was hooked.

When all the work was done, Bumper turned and headed back for the garage. While the bike cooled off in the shop, the guys had a cold drink and fixed Steve's bicycle.

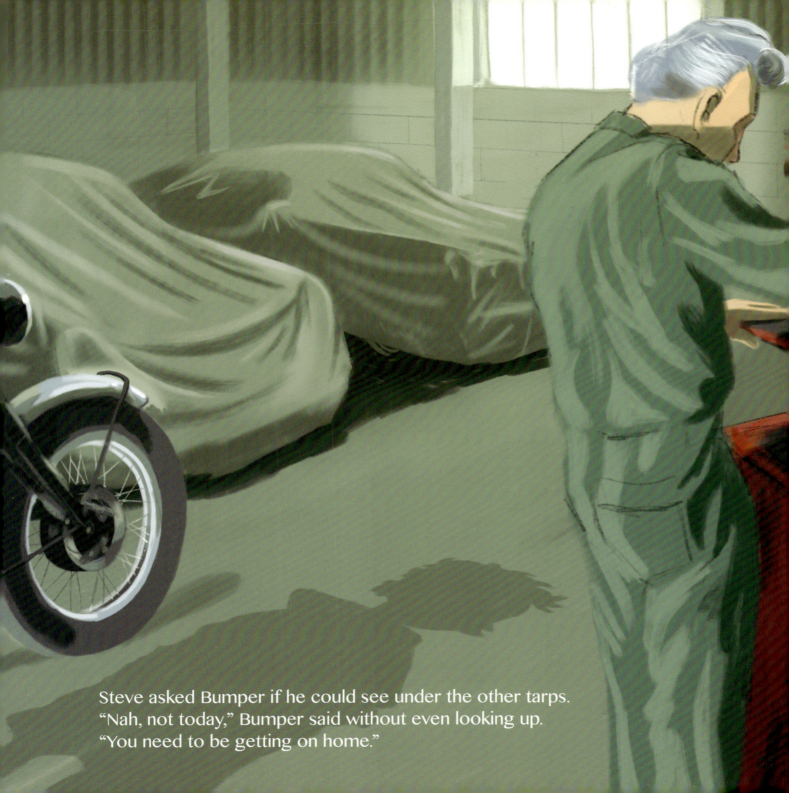
Steve asked Bumper if he could see under the other tarps.
"Nah, not today," Bumper said without even looking up.
"You need to be getting on home."

He could see the disappointment on the boy's face as he turned to go. Steve was halfway through the door when Bumper called out, "You know, if you ever get tired of that paper route, I could sure use a hand around the shop."

Back home, Steve went on and on about his day at the shop. How they had run short on time and how the motorcycle had looked and smelled and sounded. He was so excited about going to work in the shop, and he couldn't wait to see under the other tarps.

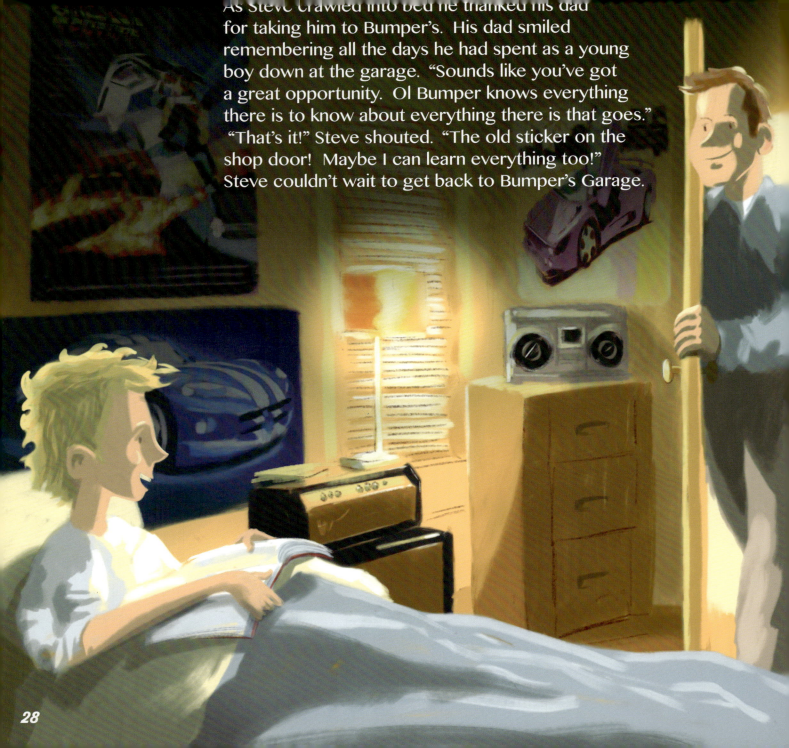

As Steve crawled into bed he thanked his dad for taking him to Bumper's. His dad smiled remembering all the days he had spent as a young boy down at the garage. "Sounds like you've got a great opportunity. Ol Bumper knows everything there is to know about everything there is that goes." "That's it!" Steve shouted. "The old sticker on the shop door! Maybe I can learn everything too!" Steve couldn't wait to get back to Bumper's Garage.

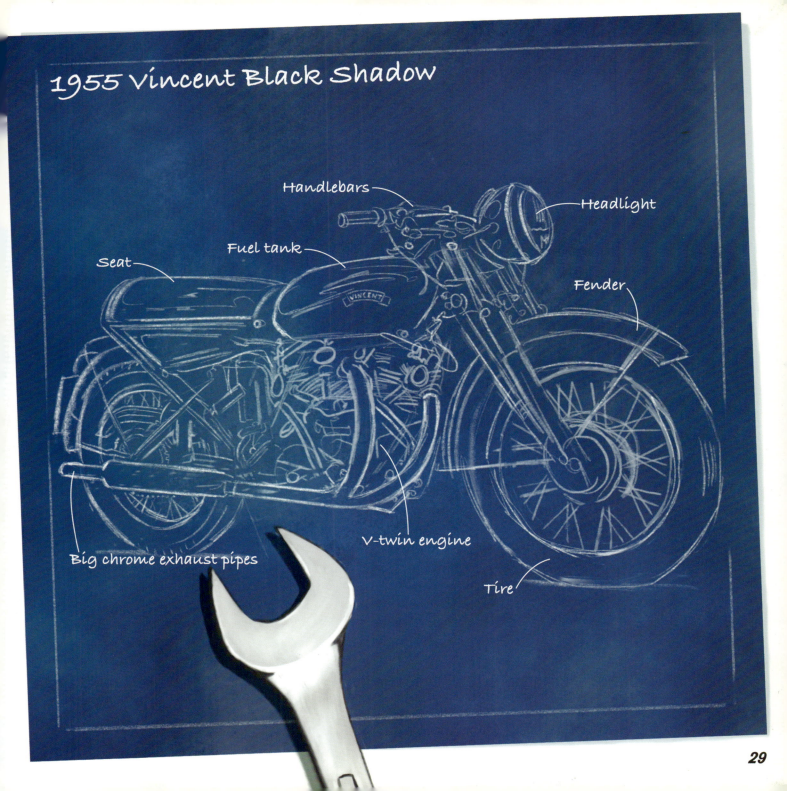